Parenting Through Milestones

A Guide to Growing Alongside Your Child

MINAKSHI PANDA

Dedication

To my parents and my kids Arunish and Aradhya, the unwavering inspiration of my life, whose teachings sparked the journey of writing this book.

And to the countless parents who strive tirelessly to nurture and support their children. May the insights within these pages be a guiding light, helping every parent find strength and clarity in their journey, free from unnecessary struggle.

Contents

Introduction

Parenting is a journey filled with wonder, responsibility, and constant change. From the first days of holding your newborn to watching them take their first steps, start school, make friends, and eventually leave home to start a life of their own, each stage brings a unique blend of joy, challenge, and growth. Parenting Through Milestones is your companion on this journey, offering guidance and insight into navigating each phase of your child's development, as well as your own growth as a parent.

In our fast-paced world, balancing work, family responsibilities, and self-care can be overwhelming. Expectations can seem endless, and societal pressures to "get it right" can leave parents feeling anxious and uncertain. This book is designed to help you find your own balance, embracing both the beautiful and the challenging aspects of parenting. As you progress through each chapter, you'll discover practical tips, real-life examples, and reflections aimed at helping you foster a strong family bond, cultivate resilience, and celebrate each milestone with confidence.

Each stage of parenting, from infancy through the teenage years and into adulthood, requires us to grow and adapt. Our children's needs evolve, and our roles shift as we transition from hands-on caregivers to supportive mentors. This book approaches each phase with empathy, acknowledging that parenting is not a one-size-fits-all experience. You'll find encouragement to develop your unique style, tune into your family's needs, and create a nurturing environment that allows everyone in the family to thrive.

Parenting Through Milestones goes beyond common advice, offering insights into topics like fostering independence, managing the complexities of work-life balance, and preparing for the empty nest. It acknowledges that while parenting can be joyful, it's also a journey of self-discovery, where we continually learn about ourselves and our children.

Whether you're facing sleepless nights with a newborn, navigating the complexities of teenage independence, or preparing to embrace the quiet of an empty nest, this book provides a roadmap for each stage. With every chapter, we hope to remind you that while challenges are inevitable, so is the profound joy that comes with watching your child grow.

May this book serve as a steady, comforting guide, offering encouragement, practical advice, and inspiration as you navigate the evolving landscape of parenthood with love and confidence. Embrace each moment, and remember that, just as much as they need us, we are learning and growing alongside our children.

Chapter 1: The Beginning of Forever: A Parent's Journey

"Parenting is a life time job and does not stop when a child grows up." –Jake Slope

Parenthood is one of life's most transformative journeys, filled with both moments of challenge and joy. The path ahead, while uncertain, is full of opportunities to grow, love, and learn. From the very first moment a child is born, parents are thrust into a world of decisions that will shape not only the child but also the parents themselves. This chapter invites you to step into the shoes of a parent on this profound adventure.

Expecting Joy
The journey begins with anticipation. As parents prepare for the arrival of their newborn, there is excitement, anxiety, and wonder. This phase is filled with doctor's visits, setting up the nursery, and attending prenatal classes, all while dreams for the future take root. The choices made during this time lay the groundwork for the adventure of parenthood. Every detail, from how you bond with your baby before birth to how you prepare emotionally, will shape the parenting experience ahead.

Nurturing Bonds
With the arrival of the baby, the real journey begins. Parenting is not just a role but a relationship, built on everyday moments of care, affection, and patience. As parents feed, change, and play with their newborn, the connection deepens. The baby's first smile, the feel of tiny hands grasping yours— these moments form the building blocks of a loving,

lifelong bond. Parents will quickly learn that how they respond to their child's needs, emotions, and cues shapes not only their development but also the dynamics of the entire family.

The Village of Support
It's often said that "it takes a village to raise a child," and this is one of the most comforting truths of parenthood. Throughout this journey, parents will rely on friends, family, and communities for advice, reassurance, and shared experiences. The joy of parenting is amplified through these connections, whether it's joining a parent's group, leaning on friends during difficult times, or celebrating milestones together. Parenthood becomes a collective adventure, one that is enriched by the love and support of those around you.

Unexpected Twists
Parenting is never without surprises. From sleepless nights to teething troubles, parents must navigate the highs and lows of family life. These unexpected twists can be both challenging and rewarding. The first few months might bring exhaustion, but they are also filled with moments of wonder—first laughs, first words, and first steps. As parents learn to adapt to the unpredictability of their child's needs, they discover strengths they never knew they had.

Educational Adventures
As the child grows, so do the opportunities for
learning and discovery. Each new stage brings
unique educational milestones, from a toddler's
curiosity to a school-aged child's first academic
achievements. Parents play a pivotal role in guiding
their child's growth, helping them explore their
interests and cultivate their talents. The joy of
watching a child develop into their own person—
curious, confident, and compassionate—is one of
the most rewarding aspects of parenthood.

Celebrating Milestones
Every family's journey is filled with milestones that
mark the passage of time and growth. Birthdays,
holidays, and achievements, both big and small, are
moments to cherish. Parents will look back on these
milestones with a sense of pride and wonder,
reflecting on how far their family has come. From
the first day of school to significant life decisions,
every step is a celebration of love and progress.

Legacy of Love
At the heart of the parenting journey is a legacy of
love. Every choice, every sacrifice, every moment
of joy and struggle weaves together the fabric of
family life. As parents witness the lasting impact of
their guidance and care, they are filled with a deep
sense of fulfillment. The bond forged through these

shared experiences becomes the cornerstone of the
family's story. As children grow into their own,
parents will look back with nostalgia, knowing that
the love and connection that shaped their family
will endure for generations.

*Parenthood is a journey that changes both parent
and child, creating a legacy of love that shapes the
future. From the first breath to the final embrace,
this adventure is one of life's most beautiful
stories.*

Chapter 2: The Architects of Childhood: Parents as Role Models

"A good father is a source of inspiration and self-restraint. A good mother is the root of kindness and humbleness." —Dr T.P.Chia

Central to effective parenting is understanding and embracing the multifaceted roles that come with it. Beyond providing for a child's physical needs, parents shape their children's character, worldview, and emotional development. This chapter explores the dynamic nature of parenthood, highlighting the importance of unity and a supportive family environment in fostering a child's growth and well-being.

Establishing Strong Connections with Your Child

Parenting is about building meaningful connections. Imagine a parent-child relationship where you're aware of how your personality influences your parenting style and how your child's personality interacts with your own. This awareness can transform the dynamic into one where both parent and child feel understood and valued, minimizing the friction caused by personality differences. Recognizing that all personalities are valid—none superior to another—enables parents to nurture their child's self-esteem and connect in ways that were previously unseen.

Changing Self-Defeating Behavior Patterns

Many parents, at some point, realize they're stuck in reactive behavior patterns. These habitual responses can stifle growth in both the parent and the child.

When parents recognize their personality strategy—
how they instinctively react to situations—they can
break free from these limiting habits and gain new
perspectives. This self-awareness helps create more
positive and effective interactions, allowing parents
to become true guides rather than dictators or
enforcers.

By stepping back from the need to dominate and
instead facilitating their child's growth, parents shift
their role. They move from being the center of
attention to becoming mentors who encourage their
children to develop into their authentic selves.
Though this shift can feel counterintuitive at first,
over time it nurtures a more balanced, affirming
relationship.

Deepening Communication with Your Child
Effective communication is the cornerstone of a
healthy parent-child relationship. However,
communication styles are heavily influenced by
personality, and a mismatch between parent and
child can lead to disconnection. Imagine trying to
explain to your child the importance of
consequences for actions, like breaking a neighbor's
window. If your child shares your personality type,
understanding will likely flow more easily. But
what about a child with a completely different
outlook? The way you communicate might actually
alienate them.

Parenting styles, often shaped by personality, vary widely:

- **Moralizers** focus on detail, analysis, and teaching morals.
- **Helpers** aim to meet the child's needs, sometimes at the expense of enforcing consequences.
- **Organizers** prefer structure, working with their child to create a clear action plan.
- **Dreamers** prioritize emotional connection and creative solutions.
- **Observers** take a big-picture view, fostering objectivity and perspective.
- **Questioners** engage through a series of mental debates, ensuring their child understands the situation logically.
- **Entertainers** are more laid-back, leaving options open for the child to choose their own path.
- **Protectors** tend to be assertive but fiercely defend their child.
- **Peacekeepers** avoid conflict, often procrastinating difficult discussions and broadening conversations to deflate tension.

By understanding your communication style, you can adjust how you interact with your child, tailoring your approach to their needs and personality.

Reducing Stress in Parent-Child Interactions
Certain interactions with your child may trigger
stress, while others bring joy. Recognizing what
causes these feelings and how your personality
plays into them is crucial. Parent-child dynamics
that consistently cause stress can lead to burnout,
but awareness allows you to shift these patterns and
cultivate more positive exchanges. Being conscious
of when you feel relaxed versus stressed helps you
manage your reactions and reduce tension in your
relationship with your child.

Gaining New Self-Awareness as a Parent
Thinking about how your personality affects your
parenting is a path to profound self-awareness.
Parenting without this knowledge is akin to
navigating in the dark, relying on instinct rather
than insight. As you become more attuned to your
motivations and behaviors, you'll better understand
your child's needs and reactions. This awareness
brings a new depth to your relationship, allowing
you to adjust your approach and become a more
thoughtful, compassionate parent.

Identifying Your Gifts, Enhancing Your Relationships

Your effectiveness as a parent is greatly enhanced when you recognize and apply your strengths. Every personality has a high and low side— situations that bring out the best or worst in us. By learning to manage your own stress and anxiety, you'll be more capable of using your gifts to foster your child's growth and to support their developing talents.

Becoming a Facilitator: Helping Your Child's Personality Flourish

Parenting with self-awareness transforms you into a facilitator of your child's development. When you understand your own motivations and tendencies, compassion naturally follows—both for yourself and for others. You begin to see your child's behavior through a more empathetic lens. By stepping back and allowing your child to express their personality, you encourage their growth in ways that are unique to them.

This process can take time and might not yield immediate results. However, staying committed to seeing both yourself and your child through the lens of personality will gradually reveal the rich patterns that make human behavior so complex and fascinating.

Getting Started
The journey to understanding your personality and that of your child is a continuous one. By learning to recognize your parenting patterns and exploring new ways to engage with your child, you'll become a more effective, empathetic parent. As you deepen your self-awareness and understanding of your child's personality, you open the door to a richer, more fulfilling relationship with them—one based on respect, understanding, and shared growth.

Parenting is not about having all the answers, but about being open to growth—both your own and your child's. By embracing the role of a facilitator, you help your child flourish into their true self, setting the stage for a lifetime of love, understanding, and mutual respect.

Chapter 3: Parenting Styles

"Parenthood…It's about guiding the next generation, and forgiving the last." –Peter Krause

No single approach to parenting fits all situations. Children are unique, and so are families. This chapter explores a variety of parenting styles, helping readers understand which approach might best suit their household dynamics. From

authoritative to permissive, each style has its strengths and potential challenges, making it crucial to recognize which method resonates with your values and your child's needs. As children grow, parents need to be flexible and adapt their styles to the evolving nature of their relationship with their children.

Authoritative Parenting

This style emphasizes balance—combining warmth, structure, and firm boundaries. Authoritative parents set clear rules but are also responsive to their children's emotional needs. This method fosters independence, self-regulation, and social competence in children. However, it requires constant reflection and adjustment to avoid becoming overly rigid or too permissive in certain situations.

Permissive Parenting : Permissive parents tend to be warm and indulgent, often avoiding conflict and allowing their children significant freedom. While this can promote creativity and self-expression, it may also result in children lacking self-discipline and struggling with boundaries. The challenge for permissive parents is finding a balance between nurturing their child's independence and ensuring they respect rules and guidelines.

Authoritarian Parenting: An authoritarian approach is characterized by strict rules and high expectations, with little room for negotiation. While it can foster discipline and respect, children raised in this environment may develop self-esteem issues or struggle with rebellion. The key for authoritarian parents is learning to incorporate emotional support while maintaining order.

Uninvolved Parenting : Uninvolved parenting is often a result of stress, work, or other challenges that prevent parents from being actively engaged. Though it may not be intentional, this approach can leave children feeling neglected and unsupported. The goal for these parents is to reconnect and rebuild the parent-child relationship.

Finding Your Style : Ultimately, no one style is the "right" one, and most parents use a combination of methods. Reflecting on your approach, adapting to your child's needs, and maintaining open communication can help you strike the right balance in your family.

Chapter 4: Building a Strong Foundation

"We must remember that one day our children are going to follow our example instead of our advice."

– Carolina King

A stable and loving home environment is essential for a child's growth and development. This chapter emphasizes the importance of creating a solid foundation based on love, traditions, and clear values. By fostering a nurturing and secure environment, parents give their children the confidence and tools needed to face life's challenges with resilience and integrity.

Family Traditions and Rituals

Family traditions provide children with a sense of continuity and belonging. Whether it's a weekly game night or special holiday celebrations, these rituals create lasting memories and strengthen familial bonds. Parents are encouraged to create traditions that reflect their values and interests, fostering a sense of identity and security within the family unit.

Instilling Values and Principles

A child's moral compass is shaped by the values and principles instilled in them at home. Whether it's honesty, kindness, or responsibility, these core values guide children's decisions and behavior throughout life. Parents must be intentional in modeling these values, demonstrating them through everyday actions and reinforcing them through positive discipline.

United We Stand, Divided We Fall

When two parents share the responsibility of raising a child, it's essential to maintain a united front. Children are keen observers and may attempt to exploit any divide between their parents to get what they want. This section provides practical tips for co-parenting effectively, ensuring both parents are aligned in their approach and maintain consistency in their rules and expectations.

- **Accept Parenting Disagreements**: It's natural for parents to disagree at times, but these differences should be handled in private. Work through them without undermining each other's authority in front of the children. Finding common ground is critical to preventing children from playing one parent against the other.
- **Communicate Privately**: Keep difficult conversations about parenting styles or decisions private, away from the children. Open discussions should be respectful and constructive, focusing on the best approach for the family's well-being.
- **Don't Let Children Divide You**: If your child tells you one parent gave them permission for something questionable (like

- ice cream for breakfast), verify the claim. If they are found to be deceitful, there should be consequences. Maintaining transparency and accountability helps uphold trust.
- **Know Each Parent's Strengths**: Every parent brings unique strengths to the table. If one parent is great at calming bedtime chaos while the other excels in creating fun weekend activities, divide responsibilities based on these strengths. Balance out the less fun jobs to avoid one parent always being the disciplinarian.
- **Encourage Breaks and Balance**: Parenting is exhausting, and it's okay to give each other a break. If one partner is having a rough day, cut them some slack and be supportive rather than critical. Both parents should feel they can rely on each other for respite and encouragement.
- **Praise Each Other's Parenting**: Acknowledge and appreciate your partner's efforts. A simple "good job" after a difficult parenting moment can go a long way in maintaining harmony. Remember, you're both on the same team, working toward the same goal: raising happy, well-adjusted children.

Chapter 5: Positive Reinforcement and Encouragement in Parenting

"If I expect my children to be kind, gentle, compassionate, and respectful, I must be kind, gentle, compassionate, and respectful. Children do not listen to the instruction of hypocrites; it is your actions that guide their actions, not your lectures or punishment." — *Rebecca Eanes*

Recognizing and Rewarding Effort
Every parent wants their child to feel loved,
supported, and motivated. But one of the most
powerful ways to build a child's confidence and
foster growth is through positive reinforcement and
encouragement. This chapter delves into the
psychology of affirming your child's efforts, rather
than focusing solely on results. When children are
praised for their effort, persistence, and strategies,
they learn the value of hard work and resilience,
even when they don't succeed right away.

*"I try to praise my daughter when she works hard at
something, even if the outcome isn't perfect.
Whether it's her school project or learning a new
skill, I let her know that the process matters more
than perfection."* —Mother of a 10-year-old

Types of Positive Reinforcement
Parents often default to tangible rewards such as
toys or treats. While these can be effective at times,
verbal praise and emotional reinforcement are
equally, if not more, impactful. Words like, "I'm
proud of you for trying so hard," or "You're getting
better every day," go a long way in shaping a
child's mindset toward learning and personal

growth. This section breaks down different types of reinforcement:

- Verbal Praise: Direct compliments that affirm the child's efforts or accomplishments.
- Physical Reinforcement: Gestures like hugs, high-fives, or a gentle pat on the back.
- Token Rewards: Using charts or stickers to visually track progress in achieving goals.
- Special Privileges: Offering additional playtime or a family outing as a reward for consistent effort.

"Whenever my son completes his homework without being asked, I give him extra time to play video games. It's our way of celebrating his responsibility." —Father of two

The Balance Between Encouragement and Overpraising
While positive reinforcement is essential, overpraising or praising the wrong behaviors can have unintended consequences. Constantly telling a child they are "so smart" for every little achievement can lead them to avoid challenges for fear of not living up to that label. The chapter explores how to strike the right balance by

encouraging effort over natural talent, thereby
promoting a growth mindset.

- Focus on improvement: "You're getting
  better at this every time!"
- Encourage persistence: "I can see you didn't
  give up, even when it got hard."
- Acknowledge struggles: "It's okay that you
  made a mistake; what's important is that
  you're learning from it."

*"When my daughter was younger, I used to tell her
she was 'perfect' at everything. As she got older, I
realized that sometimes made her scared to try new
things. Now, I praise her for trying, not for being
the best."* —Mother of a 12-year-old

Building Self-Esteem Through Encouragement
Children develop their self-esteem based on the
feedback they receive from those closest to them—
primarily their parents. This section explains how
consistent encouragement helps a child build a
strong sense of self-worth, allowing them to take on
new challenges with confidence. A child who
believes in their abilities is more likely to tackle

obstacles head-on, whether in school, sports, or
personal relationships.

*"Whenever my son feels down, I remind him of all
the things he's achieved so far. It's a great way to
lift his spirits and keep him motivated."* —Father of
a 9-year-old

Avoiding the Pitfalls of Conditional Praise
Some forms of praise can feel conditional to a
child—dependent on their success or good
behavior. This can lead to a fear of failure or a sense
of being valued only when they perform well. The
chapter discusses how to avoid this trap and instead
emphasize unconditional love and support, no
matter the outcome of their efforts.

*"I used to only praise my kids when they got good
grades. But I realized that made them afraid to
come to me when they were struggling. Now, I make
sure to support them even when things don't go as
planned."* —Mother of three

Real-Life Stories of Positive Parenting
The chapter concludes with real-life stories from
parents who have seen the benefits of positive
reinforcement in their children's lives. These

anecdotes provide practical examples of how parents can incorporate encouragement into everyday situations, from homework struggles to sibling rivalries.

"After a lot of practice, my daughter finally rode her bike without training wheels. She was so proud, but I made sure to remind her that it was her persistence that made it happen, not just the final result." —Father of a 7-year-old

Positive reinforcement is more than just a tool for shaping behavior—it's a way to build trust, self-esteem, and a healthy parent-child bond. Encouraging effort, rewarding persistence, and focusing on improveme

Chapter 6: Discipline and Boundaries

"Remember you are not managing an inconvenience. You are raising a human being."
— *Kittie Franz*

Discipline forms the backbone of effective parenting, offering structure while fostering emotional growth. In this chapter, we explore the complexities of discipline, focusing on how to set age-appropriate boundaries, balance authority with love, and create an environment where children learn responsibility, respect, and self-regulation. Discipline isn't about punishment—it's about guidance, consistency, and understanding.

The Top 10 Discipline Techniques

Although opinions on discipline can vary, there is a general consensus among experts on what makes a method effective. The aim is to teach a child to make better choices while maintaining their self-esteem and respect. Here are ten proven techniques that align with modern parenting approaches:

1. **Time-outs**
   This classic technique is ideal for younger children who need a moment to cool down. Time-outs give your child space to reflect on their behavior without feeling humiliated. The key is to stay calm, keep the duration appropriate for their age (about one minute per year of age), and explain clearly why they are in time-out.

2. **Natural Consequences**
   Letting your child experience the natural outcomes of their behavior helps them understand cause and effect. For instance, if they refuse to wear a jacket on a chilly day, they'll feel cold. As long as the consequences are safe, this method allows children to learn from their actions.
3. **Logical Consequences**
   When natural consequences aren't feasible, logical consequences provide an alternative. These are directly related to the misbehavior. For example, if your child spills their drink on purpose, a logical consequence would be having them clean it up. This teaches accountability and responsibility.
4. **Positive Reinforcement**
   Instead of focusing solely on punishing negative behaviors, emphasize rewarding positive ones. Praise or rewards for good behavior encourage your child to repeat those actions. A sticker chart for younger children or verbal praise for older ones can go a long way.
5. **Setting Clear Expectations**
   Children thrive when they know what's expected of them. Clear rules provide structure and make discipline fair. Make

sure your expectations are simple, consistent, and age-appropriate. Avoid setting too many rules, and ensure that both parents are on the same page to avoid confusion.

6. **Consistency**
   Being consistent with discipline is crucial. If your child knows that the consequences of misbehavior are predictable, they're less likely to push boundaries. Inconsistent responses can confuse children and encourage testing of limits. Always follow through on promises, whether they're about rewards or consequences.
7. **Modeling Good Behavior**
   Children are great imitators. When you model respectful, calm behavior, your child is likely to mirror it. Be mindful of how you handle stress, frustration, and conflict because your child learns more from your actions than from your words.
8. **Problem-Solving Together**
   As children grow older, involving them in finding solutions to behavior issues fosters responsibility. Ask them to come up with ways to avoid repeating the same mistake.

This not only strengthens their problem-solving skills but also gives them a sense of ownership over their actions.

9. **Offering Choices**
   Offering controlled choices empowers children without compromising parental authority. Instead of simply giving commands, ask, "Would you like to put your toys away now or after dinner?" This technique gives your child a sense of control while ensuring they meet your expectations.
10. **Time-In**
    Instead of sending your child away during moments of misbehavior, stay close and talk about what happened. A "time-in" encourages emotional connection and helps your child express their feelings constructively. This technique works particularly well with younger children who need help managing their emotions.

The Importance of Boundaries

Setting clear and age-appropriate boundaries is essential for helping your child feel safe and understand their place in the world. Boundaries should be firm but flexible enough to adapt as your child grows. A toddler might need boundaries around safety, like not touching the stove, while a preteen might need guidance around screen time and friendships.

Boundaries help children understand that certain behaviors are unacceptable, but they should always be combined with explanations. When you explain why a rule exists, your child is more likely to respect it.

Discipline with Love and Encouragement

No matter the technique you choose, discipline should always come from a place of love. Your child should never feel that their worth is tied to their behavior. Emphasize that it's the behavior, not the child, that is being corrected. Encourage them with kind words and help them understand that making mistakes is part of learning.

Tailoring Discipline to Your Child's Development

Different stages of childhood require different discipline approaches. What works for a preschooler won't necessarily be effective for a teenager. Recognize your child's developmental needs and adjust your methods accordingly. This will help you strike the right balance between nurturing independence and maintaining guidance.

Chapter 7: Nurturing Emotional Intelligence

"Don't worry that children never listen to you;
worry that they are always watching you."

– Robert Fulghum

In today's fast-paced, emotionally complex world, equipping children with emotional intelligence (EI) is essential. Children who learn to recognize and manage their emotions are better equipped to handle stress, build meaningful relationships, and approach challenges with resilience. This chapter explores the fundamentals of emotional intelligence, offering practical advice on teaching children to express themselves constructively, understand others' emotions, and develop empathy.

Why Emotional Intelligence Matters

According to a study conducted by the nonprofit think tank Public Agenda, 83% of parents believe it's important to teach children how to manage difficult emotions, but only 34% feel they've succeeded in doing so. Emotional intelligence involves understanding and controlling one's emotions, as well as recognizing and responding to the emotions of others. This skill set lays the foundation for healthy relationships and personal well-being throughout life.

Emotional intelligence can help children:

- Navigate social situations with empathy.
- Make thoughtful decisions rather than reactive ones.
- Build strong emotional connections with others.
- Handle stress, anger, and frustration constructively.

Teaching Children Emotional Awareness

The first step in nurturing emotional intelligence is helping children recognize and name their emotions. Developing a feelings vocabulary allows them to communicate their emotions more effectively, making it easier to manage those feelings. Start by teaching your child basic emotions like happiness, sadness, anger, and fear, then gradually introduce more complex terms like frustration, anxiety, or excitement.

Here is a list of words to help children expand their emotional vocabulary:

- Happy: joyful, content, delighted, proud.
- Sad: disappointed, lonely, heartbroken, and gloomy.
- Angry: irritated, furious, resentful, enraged.
- Fearful: nervous, anxious, frightened, and insecure.

- Confident: brave, courageous, bold,
  determined.

Introducing these words will empower your child to
express themselves more clearly and allow them to
better understand the emotions of those around
them.

Anger Management for Kids

Managing strong emotions like anger and
frustration can be particularly challenging for
children, but these are key emotions to address in
building emotional intelligence. Here's how you
can help your child master self-control and
emotional regulation:

1. **The Importance of Self-Control**
   Teach your child why mastering self-control
   is essential. According to Michele Borba,
   author of *Building Moral Intelligence*,
   discussing what self-control is and why it's
   important can motivate children to work on
   it. Ask your child reflective questions such
   as, "What does it mean to have good self-
   control?" and "What can people do to regain

control when they lose it?" This helps them understand the concept and how it applies in everyday situations.

2. **Normalize Frustrations**
   Let your child know that frustration is a normal part of life, and everyone—kids and adults alike—deals with it. Share examples from your own life where you experienced frustration and explain how you handled it. This can help children see that their emotions are valid and manageable. For instance, a mother shared how she told her daughter about her own frustrations while drawing Christmas cards and how she had to redo her sketches several times before being satisfied.

3. **Monitor Media Consumption**
   It's important to be mindful of the media your child consumes. TV shows, movies, and video games that glamorize losing control or violent reactions can undercut your efforts to teach emotional regulation. Be selective about what your child watches, making sure it aligns with the values you're instilling.

4. **Teach Emotional Literacy**
   Help your child develop the language to articulate their emotions. By expanding their emotional vocabulary, children can better

express their feelings and understand others' emotions. As your child becomes more familiar with expressing themselves, they might surprise you by using words like "agitated" or "apprehensive" to describe their emotions.

The Language of Feelings

Building emotional literacy is essential for helping children tune into their emotions and those of others. Introducing your child to new words related to emotions allows them to better articulate how they feel. Here are some words to add to their emotional vocabulary:

- **Excited:** thrilled, energetic, exhilarated.
- **Scared:** worried, frightened, petrified.
- **Proud:** accomplished, fulfilled, satisfied.
- **Frustrated:** irritated, baffled, discouraged.
- **Curious:** intrigued, fascinated, inquisitive.

By regularly introducing and discussing these words, you're helping your child become more adept at managing and expressing their emotions.

Fostering Empathy and Compassion

Empathy is a crucial aspect of emotional intelligence. It involves recognizing and understanding the feelings of others. You can nurture empathy in your child by modeling compassionate behavior and discussing the emotions and experiences of others.

1. **Model Empathy**
    Children learn empathy by observing how you respond to others. When they see you comforting a friend, being patient with a stranger, or expressing concern for others, they are more likely to replicate those behaviors.
2. **Teach Perspective-Taking**
    Encourage your child to put themselves in someone else's shoes. Ask them questions like, "How do you think your friend felt when you said that?" or "What would you do if you were in their situation?" This helps them develop the ability to understand others' emotions.
3. **Promote Acts of Kindness**
    Engaging your child in simple acts of kindness—like sharing, helping a friend, or being polite—can foster compassion and teach them the value of being considerate of others' feelings.

Emotional Regulation in Everyday Life

Emotional intelligence isn't something that develops overnight. It requires practice, patience, and consistency. Help your child by guiding them through everyday challenges in an emotionally intelligent way.

- **Talk About Emotions Regularly**
  Make it a habit to check in on how your child is feeling. Ask open-ended questions, like, "How did that make you feel?" and listen attentively to their responses. Over time, this will encourage open communication about emotions.
- **Model Healthy Coping Strategies**
  Children learn by watching how their parents cope with stress and difficult emotions. When you feel overwhelmed, show your child how to handle those feelings constructively—whether it's by taking a deep breath, going for a walk, or talking things out.
- **Validate Their Feelings**
  It's essential to validate your child's emotions rather than dismiss or minimize them. Let them know it's okay to feel sad,

angry, or frustrated. By validating their emotions, you teach them that it's normal to feel a wide range of emotions and that they are capable of managing them.

Chapter: 8 Managing Anger and Emotional Regulation in Children

"You do not have to make your children into wonderful people. You just have to remind them that they are wonderful people." – William Martin

Helping children understand and manage their emotions, especially strong emotions like anger, is essential for their emotional development. Anger is a natural response to certain situations, but when left unchecked, it can lead to undesirable behavior. In this chapter, we will explore practical strategies to help children manage their anger in healthy and constructive ways.

Acknowledge Your Child's Feelings

One of the most effective ways to help your child manage anger is by acknowledging their feelings. When children feel heard and understood, they are more likely to calm down. On the contrary, if they feel that no one is paying attention to their emotions, their frustration can escalate quickly.

Let your child know you understand their feelings by saying things like:

- "I can see that you're really upset right now."
- "I know this is hard for you."

This validation lets your child know that their feelings are important and real, which can deescalate a tense situation.

Teaching Children to Recognize the Physical Signs of Anger

Helping children recognize the physical sensations associated with anger is crucial in teaching them to manage their emotions before they reach a boiling point. By identifying the early signs of anger, children can learn to pause and take control before they react impulsively.

Here are some questions you can ask your child to help them recognize these signs:

- Does your heart feel like you've been running a race?
- Do you feel like you want to hit something or someone?
- Are your fists clenched tightly?
- Does your body feel tense or stiff?
- Are you breathing faster than usual?
- Do the muscles in your face feel tight?
- Are your eyes squinted together?

As a parent, you may also need to observe these signs and point them out to your child until they become adept at recognizing them independently.

Once they're able to identify these signals, they can begin to take steps to calm down.

The Importance of Self-Control

Emotionally intelligent individuals are better equipped to cope with their emotions and are less likely to turn to negative outlets, such as substance abuse, later in life. They also tend to have healthier relationships because they are more attuned to the emotions of others. Teaching self-control at an early age can have long-term positive effects both personally and professionally.

Encouraging a Pause Before Reacting

It's essential to remind children that they don't have to react to situations immediately. Teach them to take a moment to think about the consequences of their actions before reacting. This pause gives them time to cool down and make better decisions.

Encourage them to:

- Take a few deep breaths.
- Walk away from the situation if they feel too upset.
- Think about what might happen if they react in a certain way.

This approach helps children learn to manage their emotions rather than being overwhelmed by them.

Setting Clear Standards for Managing Anger

Children need clear boundaries when it comes to expressing anger. Let your child know that while it's okay to feel angry, certain behaviors are unacceptable. For example:

- Hitting others is not an option.
- Name-calling or verbal abuse is not allowed.
- Throwing things or having a tantrum is inappropriate.

Once these standards are established, consistently reinforce them. Help your child understand that they are expected to express their anger in healthier ways.

Physical Outlets for Anger

Physical activity is an excellent way for children to release pent-up anger and stress. If you notice that your child is having a particularly bad day, suggest a physical activity, such as:

- Playing a game of basketball.
- Going for a walk or a run.
- Dancing or jumping on a trampoline.

These activities provide a safe outlet for anger while helping children discover how exercise can positively impact their mood and stress levels.

Deep Breathing for Stress Relief

Deep breathing is a simple but effective technique for calming down when feeling overwhelmed by anger. Teach your child how to take deep, slow breaths to relax their body and mind.

A fun way to demonstrate deep breathing to younger children is by using bubble-blowing solution. Explain that the slow, steady breaths needed to blow the biggest bubbles are the same type of breaths they should take when they're feeling upset. This visual and interactive approach makes the concept more tangible and easier to grasp for young children.

Helping Children Put Their Feelings into Words

If your child is struggling to express their feelings, help them find the words to describe what they're experiencing. Sometimes children act out in anger because they can't articulate what they're feeling.

Use questions like:

- "Are you feeling frustrated because you didn't get your way?"
- "Do you feel sad that your friend didn't want to play with you?"

By helping them identify their emotions, you provide them with the tools they need to communicate their feelings effectively, reducing the likelihood of emotional outbursts.

Chapter 9: Educational Support

"If your children fear you, they cannot trust you. If they don't trust you, they cannot learn from you."

— Lori Petro

Parents play a crucial role in supporting their children's educational journey. This chapter provides guidance on creating an environment that fosters a love for learning, collaborating with teachers, and actively participating in a child's academic development. By understanding the brain's role in learning, parents can better assist their children in transforming information into knowledge.

RAD Learning: Reticular Activating System + Amygdala's Filter + Dopamine

1. **R = Reticular Activating System (RAS):** The RAS helps the brain decide which information to focus on. Parents can stimulate the RAS through mindful focus activities, changes in the environment, and multisensory lessons. This part of the brain is responsible for filtering sensory input and directing attention toward what it perceives as important—whether for survival or pleasure. Using teachable moments, parents can help trigger this brain mechanism to enhance their child's ability to engage with new information.
2. **A = Amygdala:** The amygdala is sensitive to stress and emotional stimuli. Games and activities that

reduce stress and build positive associations with learning keep this filter open to higher brain functions. If learning is fun, the amygdala helps imprint that experience into long-term memory. Stress, boredom, or frustration, however, will cause it to block new information. Therefore, helping children associate learning with curiosity and success enhances retention and emotional engagement.

3. **D = Dopamine:**
   Dopamine, a neurotransmitter linked to pleasure and reward, is released when the brain anticipates enjoyable experiences. Activities that engage a child's interests and stimulate a sense of accomplishment promote dopamine release, which improves focus, attention, and executive function. Using neurological strategies to accelerate learning, such as gamified tasks, can leverage dopamine's effects to enhance performance.

Helping Your Child Turn Information into Knowledge

Parents can assist their children in developing personalized strategies that align with their learning strengths. By establishing clear goals, parents can guide their children's academic growth in specific areas. Common goals might include:

- Building a joyful, successful approach to learning
- Strengthening self-esteem and confidence
- Encouraging self-motivation and organizational strategies
- Enhancing performance on tests and homework
- Promoting curiosity and creativity in problem-solving
- Developing mindfulness and healthy study habits
- Stimulating a wide range of interests, from academics to extracurricular

Once parents have identified their child's strengths, they can use this book's brain-friendly approaches to nurture those skills and maximize their child's potential.

The Science Behind Better Learning

The interaction between the RAS, amygdala, and dopamine forms a powerful triad for learning. When parents understand how these systems work together, they can create an environment that enhances their child's ability to absorb and retain knowledge. Encouraging positive emotional experiences, reducing stress, and reinforcing pleasure-driven learning are key elements in fostering long-term academic success.

Sharing Strengths and Strategies with Your Child's Teachers

If there's a mismatch between a child's learning strengths and the type of instruction they receive at school, it can result in frustration, underachievement, or even misdiagnosis of learning disorders like ADHD or dyslexia. Parents can act as advocates by informing teachers about their child's preferred learning style, leading to adjustments that better suit the child's needs. For example:

- Suggest alternatives for homework that cater to your child's strengths (e.g., creating stories with vocabulary words instead of copying definitions).
- Offer insights into how your child learns best, which can help teachers re-evaluate any labels or behaviors that might have been misunderstood.

Discovering Your Child's Learning Strengths

There are two major classifications of learning
strengths covered in this chapter, which encompass
elements of both **Multiple Intelligences** and
Learning Styles:

1. **Visual-Spatial-Kinesthetic (VSK)
    Learners:**
    These learners process information through
    images, movement, and spatial relationships.
    They thrive when learning is hands-on,
    visually stimulating, and exploratory. VSK
    learners benefit from activities such as:
    * Diagrams, models, maps, and visual
      aids
    * Hands-on learning, such as
      experiments or crafting
    * Visualization techniques and
      memory strategies involving imagery
    * Movement-based learning (e.g.,
      acting out concepts or building
      models)

Challenges for VSK learners:

- ❖ Difficulty focusing during passive learning
- ❖ Trouble organizing time or communicating visual concepts verbally

2. **Auditory-Sequential (AS) Learners:**
AS learners excel in structured, logical environments. They prefer order, sequence, and auditory information. These learners are often analytical thinkers who enjoy solving problems methodically. AS learners benefit from:

- ❖ Clear instructions, logical sequences, and structured activities
- ❖ Verbal explanations, audiobooks, and quizzes
- ❖ Graphic organizers, timelines, and compare-contrast activities
- ❖ Memorization techniques like mnemonics or reading aloud

Challenges for AS learners:

- ❖ Difficulty grasping big-picture concepts before understanding the details
- ❖ Struggling with abstract, nonverbal concepts and spatial relationships

By understanding these learning strengths, parents can adapt their approach to support their child more effectively. Additionally, when these insights are shared with teachers, it allows for better classroom adaptations, improving the overall learning experience.

Multiple Intelligences

Howard Gardner's theory of **Multiple Intelligences** suggests that intelligence is multi-faceted, and everyone possesses a unique combination of these strengths. The most relevant for understanding your child's learning preferences include:

- **Linguistic intelligence:** Proficiency with language and words
- **Logical-mathematical intelligence:** Ability to work with patterns, sequences, and logic
- **Musical-rhythmic intelligence:** Sensitivity to sound and rhythm

- **Visual-spatial intelligence:** Skills in visualization and spatial reasoning
- **Bodily-kinesthetic intelligence:** Coordination and learning through movement
- **Interpersonal intelligence:** Sensitivity to others' feelings and emotions
- **Intrapersonal intelligence:** Self-reflection and understanding
- **Naturalist intelligence:** Awareness of and appreciation for nature

Evaluating Your Child's Learning Strengths

To better understand how your child learns, observe their preferences during everyday activities. Does your child enjoy problem-solving through experimentation, or do they prefer a more methodical, step-by-step approach? By tapping into your child's natural strengths, you can help them find greater joy and success in their educational journey.

Chapter 10: Technology, Parenting, and Child Psychology

In today's digital age, parenting goes beyond traditional concerns and now involves navigating the ever-evolving world of technology. This chapter explores the unique challenges posed by screen

time, how to set appropriate boundaries, and the importance of instilling responsible online behavior in children. It also delves into understanding your child's personality type and how this impacts their interaction with both technology and the world around them.

The Digital Landscape: Challenges and Opportunities

As parents, we must understand how technology affects our children both positively and negatively. Technology can be a powerful educational tool, but excessive screen time or unmonitored internet access can result in developmental concerns. To help guide your child through these challenges, it's important to:

1. **Set Clear Screen Time Limits:** Excessive screen time has been linked to issues such as sleep disruption, attention problems, and reduced physical activity. Set limits based on your child's age and developmental needs. For younger children, focus on

educational content, while for older kids, ensure a balance between recreational and productive screen use.
2. **Monitor Content and Online Behavior:** Help your child develop responsible online behavior by educating them about privacy, cyberbullying, and the importance of respectful communication. Use parental control features and regularly check their online activity to ensure safety without invading their privacy.
3. **Encourage Tech-Free Zones and Times:** Establish screen-free areas, like the dining table, and tech-free times, like during family outings. This promotes meaningful family interactions and ensures your child is not overly dependent on technology for entertainment or communication.

Your Child's Personality and Technology Use

Understanding your child's temperament helps tailor your approach to technology and parenting. Each child interacts with the digital world in ways that reflect their unique personality. The basic temperament types described by psychologists Alexander Thomas and Stella Chess offer insight into how to guide your child in this area:

1. **The Spirited Child:** This child has a higher intensity and energy level, struggles with adapting to change, and may show frustration when limits are set on technology use. With spirited children, it's essential to offer structured tech time, channeling their energy into creative or interactive apps and games that challenge their minds while keeping limits in place.
2. **The Shy Child:** Slow to warm up to new situations, this child may use technology as a comfort zone, avoiding face-to-face interactions. These children benefit from gradual exposure to technology in social contexts, like virtual classrooms or collaborative online games that foster interaction with peers without overwhelming them.
3. **The Easy Child:** Adaptable and generally positive, the easy child may be more flexible with screen time limits. However, even with their adaptability, it's important to ensure that tech use doesn't replace other valuable activities like outdoor play, reading, or family time.

Key Characteristics of Temperament

When considering your child's relationship with technology, it's helpful to understand these key aspects of their temperament:

- **Energy Level:** Does your child seem to have boundless energy and find it hard to sit still, or are they more content with quiet activities like reading or drawing? Highly energetic children might be drawn to fast-paced video games, so it's important to find active, physical outlets for their energy, such as outdoor play or interactive tech that promotes movement, like dance or fitness games.
- **Regularity of Patterns:** Does your child stick to consistent routines when it comes to eating, sleeping, and daily activities, or are they more spontaneous and erratic? Children with irregular patterns may struggle with tech-related distractions before bedtime or may need more structure to prevent technology from disrupting their sleep and overall routine.
- **Approach and Withdrawal:** How does your child react to new experiences, including new tech platforms or gadgets? Do

they eagerly embrace change, or are they more hesitant? Children who struggle with newness may benefit from gradual introduction to new apps, ensuring that tech use remains a positive experience rather than a source of anxiety.

Instilling Responsible Online Behavior

Teaching your child how to behave responsibly online is just as important as teaching them how to behave in the real world. Here's how you can help:

- **Set Clear Boundaries and Rules:** Make sure your child knows what is and isn't acceptable behavior online. This includes treating others with respect, protecting personal information, and understanding the consequences of inappropriate behavior.
- **Model Good Behavior:** Children often mirror their parents' behaviors. Set an example by managing your own screen time responsibly, practicing safe browsing habits, and being mindful of how you use technology around them.
- **Open Communication:** Encourage your child to talk to you about their online experiences. Discuss potential risks, such as

cyberbullying, and how to handle situations they might encounter online. Make sure they feel comfortable coming to you if they ever feel unsafe.

Balanced Nutrition and Technology

In the age of digital distractions, it's important to maintain a healthy balance between physical well-being and screen time. Here are some practical tips for fostering that balance:

- **Provide Balanced Nutrition:** A well-balanced diet is essential for maintaining energy levels and supporting cognitive development. Encourage meals rich in fruits, vegetables, whole grains, lean proteins, and dairy, while limiting processed foods and sugary snacks.
- **Encourage Physical Activity:** To combat the sedentary nature of screen use, ensure your child gets regular physical exercise. Encourage outdoor play, sports, or family fitness activities that counterbalance time spent sitting in front of a screen.
- **Hydration Matters:** Make sure your child stays hydrated, especially during long sessions of screen use, as dehydration can

contribute to fatigue and reduced concentration.

Conclusion: Parenting in the Digital Era

Parenting in the digital age comes with its own set of challenges, but understanding your child's temperament, guiding their tech usage, and fostering responsible online behavior can create a balanced environment for growth and development. Technology, when used mindfully, can be an excellent tool for learning and creativity. However, maintaining boundaries, promoting healthy habits, and supporting emotional and psychological well-being are key to raising well-rounded individuals in a tech-driven world.

Chapter 11: Sibling Dynamics

Fostering positive relationships among siblings is essential for a harmonious family life. This chapter delves into strategies for encouraging cooperation, addressing conflicts, and ensuring a fair distribution of attention and resources among siblings.

The Ideal Sibling Bond vs. Reality

When deciding to have more than one child, most parents envision their kids as built-in playmates and confidantes. In an ideal world, siblings share without bickering, never argue over small things, and always show support for one another. However, most families experience a reality far from this dream, where disputes over TV time, toys, or even whose turn it is on the computer become frequent.

In the past, parents were advised to ignore sibling spats, seeing them as normal childhood behavior. But modern parenting approaches recommend more active involvement, especially when fights turn nasty or emotionally damaging.

Why Sibling Relationships Can Be a Minefield for Parents

Knowing when and how to intervene in sibling conflicts can be challenging. Parents are emotionally invested in both children, which can make it difficult to remain objective. Acting as a referee often backfires, as parents might unintentionally side with one child based on who made the more compelling argument or got to them first. Without witnessing every part of the conflict, it's hard to assess the situation accurately. Trying to determine intent, such as whether a child deliberately threw a toy at a sibling, can feel like a courtroom drama.

Mother Wisdom:
"Refuse to play the blame game. If your children are fighting, don't waste your energy trying to figure out who started it. It takes two to tango."

Handling Sibling Conflicts

Rather than acting as the constant referee, parenting experts recommend allowing siblings to resolve their conflicts independently as much as possible. This promotes problem-solving skills that will benefit them throughout life. However, this doesn't mean parents should ignore everything; instead, they should coach children on how to navigate disagreements fairly and respectfully.

Some conflicts require parental mediation, especially if one child is significantly younger or if a serious issue arises. But for day-to-day squabbles, parents should encourage their children to talk through their differences and reach compromises on their own.

Strategies for Conflict Resolution

1. **Listen to Both Sides**: When a conflict
    arises, let each child explain their side of the
    story.
2. **Encourage Problem-Solving**: Guide your
    kids through brainstorming solutions that are
    acceptable to both. For example, if they're
    arguing over who ate a chocolate bar,
    suggest they check for another chocolate bar
    in the fridge, or figure out a way to replace
    it.
3. **Teach Mediation Skills**: Over time, kids
    can learn to resolve their issues without
    needing parental intervention. Encourage
    them to express their feelings calmly and to
    listen to each other's perspectives.

Mother Wisdom:
*"Don't try to give your kids a primer in conflict
resolution when they're on the verge of coming to
blows. Instead, wait until they've both had a chance
to cool down before starting the discussion."*

Promoting Healthy Sibling Relationships

While managing conflicts is essential, fostering a positive relationship between siblings goes beyond just addressing fights. Here are some ways parents can promote a healthy bond:

- **Avoid Comparisons**: Resist the urge to compare one child's behavior or achievements with another's. This can sow resentment and create competition between siblings.
- **Show Fairness, Not Equality**: Understand that fairness doesn't always mean treating children exactly the same. Each child has unique needs, and fairness often involves addressing those individual needs, not simply splitting everything down the middle.

Mother Wisdom:
"In my experience, the root of most of my children's conflicts is their perception of 'fairness.' I try to remember something my sister-in-law once said: 'Fair doesn't always mean equal.'"

- **Value Each Child's Strengths**: Acknowledge and celebrate the unique qualities of each child, helping them feel confident and valued in their own right, rather than competing for attention.
- **Teach Respect for Space and Belongings**: Establish clear boundaries about personal spaces and possessions. Siblings should

learn to respect each other's rooms,
belongings, and personal boundaries.

Consequences and Ground Rules

It's important to set clear ground rules for how
siblings should treat each other and to enforce
consequences for breaking those rules. For example,
physical violence or name-calling should have firm,
non-negotiable consequences.

Conclusion: Building Lifelong Bonds

Sibling relationships are complex, but with
patience, guidance, and the right approach, parents
can help foster a bond that will last a lifetime.
Teaching children to resolve conflicts, appreciate
each other's differences, and show respect helps lay
the foundation for a supportive and loving sibling
relationship—one that will carry through to
adulthood.

By nurturing this bond, parents not only reduce day-
to-day friction but also give their children a
priceless gift: the companionship of a lifelong
friend in their sibling.

Mother Wisdom:
*"Raising siblings is like growing a garden—each
child needs different amounts of attention, care, and
love, but with time, patience, and guidance, they'll
bloom beautifully together."*

Chapter 12: Healthy Lifestyle Habits

Promoting physical health and well-being is a fundamental aspect of parenting. This chapter delves into the importance of balanced nutrition, regular exercise, and the cultivation of healthy lifestyle habits that contribute to a child's overall well-being.

The Cycle of Care: Essential Infant-Care Skills

For new parents, especially dads, learning key skills to care for their infant can create a nurturing environment while also sharing responsibilities equally with their partner. Five crucial skills help form the foundation of care for newborns:

1. **Feeding**: Babies often feed on demand, and this requires being attuned to their needs. Whether it's expressed breast milk or formula, holding your baby close and supporting their head during feeding ensures comfort and bonding. For new parents, practicing with dolls before birth can help ease the transition to real feeding scenarios.
2. **Burping**: Air swallowed during feeding needs to be released gently. This is achieved by holding the baby upright and applying light pressure to the abdomen while patting the back rhythmically. This simple act promotes comfort after a big meal.
3. **Comforting**: Diaper changes provide an opportunity for social interaction and comfort. Frequent changes also protect the skin and prevent diaper rashes. Remember, girls should be wiped front to back to avoid infection, and for boys, have a cloth handy to guard against accidental splashes.

4. **Resting**: Babies need a significant amount of sleep, often up to 14 to 20 hours a day in the first few months. Creating a soothing environment to lull the baby into sleep is essential for their development—and for parents to catch up on rest themselves.
5. **Handling Crying**: Babies cry to communicate, and part of parenting is learning to soothe them by identifying and addressing common discomforts—hunger, fatigue, dirty diapers, or overstimulation. Understanding that crying is a normal part of communication helps build trust.

These skills help parents become active, nurturing partners, enhancing the parent-child bond and sharing the joys of care. Fathers in particular benefit from mastering these tasks, contributing to both their child's emotional development and their partner's well-being.

The Importance of Touch and Emotional Availability

The way parents handle their children physically plays a key role in their emotional and psychological development. A loving touch, whether it's cuddling, holding, or soothing, builds trust and reinforces the child's sense of security.

From infancy through childhood, physical closeness, like cuddles, often does more to comfort children than words can. As children grow, emotional availability and warm responses to their needs create a foundation for healthy emotional development. Parents who pick up their crying baby or comfort a pouting toddler demonstrate that they are reliable sources of love and support.

Emotional availability may come more naturally to mothers, given their deeper physical connection during pregnancy, but it's crucial for fathers too. Being in tune with a child's emotional cues—when they need comfort or when they are overstimulated—helps reduce stress and promotes brain development. When parents learn to respond to their baby's subtle signals, they create an environment of trust, love, and security.

Diet and Nutrition

Establishing healthy dietary habits from an early age is essential for a child's growth and well-being:

- **Balanced Diet**: Include a variety of fruits, vegetables, whole grains, lean proteins, and dairy in your child's meals.
- **Limit Sugary Snacks**: Reducing sugary foods and processed snacks can help prevent childhood obesity and promote healthy eating habits.
- **Hydration**: Encourage drinking water throughout the day, especially during physical activities, while limiting sugary drinks like soda and fruit juices.

As children grow older, parents need to adjust their meal plans to introduce solids and create mealtime routines that foster good nutrition. Discussions between parents about the role of food—whether it's nutrition, a social experience, or even a reward—help create consistency at home.

Regular Physical Activity

Physical activity is crucial for children's physical development and overall health. Encourage at least 60 minutes of moderate to vigorous exercise daily. Activities can include:

- Sports
- Outdoor play
- Dancing
- Biking

Limiting screen time is essential to encourage physical movement and prevent sedentary habits. Active children are healthier, more focused, and less prone to behavioral issues.

Adequate Sleep

Sleep is a vital component of a healthy lifestyle. Consistent sleep routines promote proper growth and mental development. For infants and children:

- Establish a bedtime routine to encourage enough rest.
- Create a calm, sleep-friendly environment by keeping electronic devices out of the bedroom.

Proper rest ensures that children are mentally sharp, emotionally stable, and physically healthy.

Good Hygiene Practices

Instilling good hygiene habits is a cornerstone of healthy living:

- **Handwashing**: Teach children proper handwashing techniques to prevent illness.
- **Dental Care**: Encourage regular tooth brushing and dentist visits to maintain oral health.
- **Personal Cleanliness**: Daily baths or showers help prevent infections and promote cleanliness.

Developing these habits from a young age encourages lifelong hygiene.

Mental Health and Emotional Well-being

A child's mental health is as important as their physical health. Parents can foster emotional well-being by:

- Encouraging open communication.
- Providing a safe space for children to express their emotions.
- Teaching mindfulness and relaxation techniques to manage stress.

Supporting mental health from an early age promotes emotional resilience and healthy coping mechanisms.

Limiting Screen Time : Screen time is a major factor in children's modern lives, but too much can be detrimental to both physical and mental health. Establish clear guidelines, encouraging educational content and limiting overall time spent on screens. Balance screen time with physical and social activities.

Positive Social Interaction: Encouraging social skills is crucial for emotional and behavioral development. Through playdates, group activities, or team sports, children learn to:

- Cooperate
- Show empathy
- Build friendships

Fostering kindness and respect for others enhances a child's social well-being.

Regular Health Check-ups : Regular pediatrician visits ensure that children are on track with their growth, development, and vaccinations. Early intervention can address health concerns promptly, safeguarding long-term well-being.

Chapter 13: Challenges and Milestones

"To be in your children's memories tomorrow, you have to be in their lives today." – *Barbara Johnson*

Parenting is a dynamic and ever-evolving journey, filled with both challenges and significant milestones. Every stage of a child's growth brings unique experiences, from navigating early childhood to guiding them through adolescence and beyond. This chapter provides insights into common challenges parents face and emphasizes the importance of celebrating key milestones that mark a child's growth and development.

Challenges:

1. **Sleep Deprivation:**
   - ❖ One of the most common challenges, particularly in the early years, is sleep deprivation. Nighttime feedings, diaper changes, and comforting a fussy baby can lead to fragmented sleep, leaving parents physically and emotionally exhausted.
2. **Balancing Work and Family:**
   - ❖ Many parents struggle with the demands of their careers while trying to meet the needs of their family. This balance can feel overwhelming at times, leading to stress and feelings of being stretched too thin.

3. **Discipline and Boundaries:**
   * Finding the right approach to discipline, setting clear boundaries, and maintaining a positive relationship with your child can be difficult. Each child is different, and what works for one may not work for another.

4. **Teenage Rebellion:**
   * The teenage years often bring a desire for independence, and with it comes the occasional rebellion. Navigating this period requires patience and understanding as parents and teens learn to communicate and compromise.

5. **Financial Strain:**
   * Raising a family can be expensive, and unexpected costs, whether they be medical, educational, or related to extracurricular activities, can add financial pressure.

6. **Time Management:**
   * Parents often juggle multiple responsibilities: work, household chores, children's activities, and personal time. Effective time management is crucial, yet challenging, as priorities shift daily.

7. **Parental Guilt:**
  - ❖ Many parents experience feelings of guilt, whether it's from not spending enough time with their children or feeling like they aren't making the right decisions. This emotional burden can be hard to shake.
8. **Peer Pressure and External Influences:**
  - ❖ As children grow older, they encounter peer pressure and external influences that may conflict with the values taught at home. Helping children navigate these pressures can be a difficult task for parents.
9. **Health Concerns:**
  - ❖ Dealing with a child's health issues or chronic conditions can be emotionally and physically draining. Parents often feel a sense of helplessness when they cannot immediately "fix" their child's problems.
10. **Technology and Screen Time:**
  - ❖ Managing the increasing role of technology in children's lives, especially with the growing influence of social media and video games, is a modern-day challenge. Parents must set boundaries while ensuring their children use technology in a healthy, balanced way.

Milestones:

First Steps and Words:

- ❖ The excitement of seeing your child take their first steps or hearing their first words is a joyous and significant milestone in early childhood. These moments mark the beginning of physical and verbal independence.

2. **Starting School:**
   - ❖ The day a child enters school is a major milestone, signaling their first formal step into education and social interaction beyond the family circle. It's a day of pride and emotional adjustment for both parents and children.

3. **Independence and Self-Care:**
   - ❖ As children grow, they begin to master essential self-care skills, such as dressing themselves, brushing their teeth, and tying their shoes. These moments are small but meaningful steps toward independence.

4. **Achievements and Awards:**
   - ❖ Whether academic, athletic, or artistic, celebrating a child's achievements shows the results of

their hard work and dedication. These moments build confidence and reinforce a sense of accomplishment.

5. **Teen Milestones:**
   * The teenage years bring several major milestones, such as a child's first job, obtaining a driver's license, and graduation. These milestones symbolize a growing sense of responsibility and personal growth.

6. **Transition to Adulthood:**
   * Guiding a child as they transition into adulthood—whether through higher education, entering the workforce, or other endeavors—is a major milestone for both the child and the parent. It's a time of reflection, pride, and preparation for the next chapter.

7. **Grandparenting:**
   * Becoming a grandparent brings the parenting journey full circle. Seeing the next generation grow and develop adds a new level of joy and meaning to life, as the family legacy continues.

8. **Establishing Values:**
   * Watching a child grow into someone who embodies the values of empathy, integrity, and kindness is perhaps one of the most rewarding milestones. It reflects not only their

growth but the impact of a parent's guidance and influence.

9. **Building Relationships:**
   - ❖ As children grow into adolescence and adulthood, developing a strong, trusting, and open relationship becomes a significant achievement. Maintaining this connection is one of the key foundations of lifelong parenting.

10. **Empty Nest:**
    - ❖ The day children leave home for college, work, or to start families of their own marks a bittersweet milestone for parents. Adjusting to an empty nest involves redefining roles and responsibilities, but it also offers an opportunity for personal growth and rediscovery.

Navigating the Journey:

Parenting is filled with highs and lows. Each challenge is an opportunity for growth, and every milestone is a reminder of the beauty and purpose of the journey. While every family's path is unique, the common thread is the love, patience, and dedication that shapes the parent-child relationship. Embracing challenges and celebrating milestones helps foster resilience and joy in both parents and children, creating lasting memories that will be cherished for a lifetime.

Chapter 14: Balancing Work and Family

Harmony at Home: Navigating the Delicate Balance

As modern life becomes more complex and demanding, balancing work and family has emerged as one of the most significant challenges parents

face. The pressures of career aspirations and personal responsibilities often create a delicate balancing act. This chapter offers practical strategies for finding harmony, ensuring that work-life balance is not just a dream but an achievable goal.

Understanding the Challenge of Work-Family Balance

Balancing work and family is not just about dividing time between the two; it is about finding a sense of equilibrium where neither your career nor your family is neglected. Parents often face competing demands, from deadlines at work to children's school activities, and managing these conflicting responsibilities can create stress and exhaustion. However, striking the right balance fosters a healthy, fulfilling life for both you and your family.**Practical Strategies for Managing Work and Family**

1. **Set Boundaries:**
    - ❖ Establish clear boundaries between work and home life. This could mean avoiding work-related tasks during family time or setting specific work hours that you adhere to when working from home. Having boundaries helps in maintaining a mental separation between work stress and family relaxation.
2. **Prioritize Quality Time:**
    - ❖ While it's easy to get caught up in the day-to-day hustle, it's essential to carve out quality time for your children and spouse. Schedule dedicated time for family activities, whether it's a weekend outing or an evening meal together. Consistent, focused time builds strong family bonds and communicates that they are your priority.
3. **Embrace Flexible Work Options:**
    - ❖ If possible, explore flexible work options such as remote work or flexible hours. Many companies are increasingly offering these benefits, which can help reduce stress by allowing you to better manage your time between work tasks and family responsibilities.
4. **Delegate and Share Responsibilities:**
    - ❖ Avoid the temptation to "do it all." Delegate responsibilities at home,

whether it's sharing chores with your spouse or involving your children in age-appropriate tasks. At work, don't hesitate to seek support from your colleagues or subordinates when needed. Learning to delegate helps lighten your load and frees up more time for what matters most.

5. **Use Technology Wisely:**
   * While technology can be a distraction, it can also be a powerful tool for staying organized. Utilize scheduling apps, reminders, and family management tools to keep track of everyone's activities. Plan and set reminders for work deadlines and family obligations, so nothing falls through the cracks.

6. **Communicate Openly:**
   * Open communication is key to balancing work and family. Have regular conversations with your spouse and children about your work commitments and family needs. Understanding each other's schedules and stressors helps in managing expectations and reducing conflict.

Fostering a Supportive Work-Life Balance

1. **Build a Support System:**
   - ❖ It's okay to ask for help. Whether it's grandparents, friends, or hired help, building a support network eases the load of parenting. Consider options like after-school programs or part-time childcare services to manage the gap between work hours and family time.
2. **Use Family-Friendly Benefits:**
   - ❖ Take advantage of family-friendly benefits that your workplace may offer, such as parental leave, on-site childcare, or wellness programs. Knowing your rights and options can make a significant difference in creating a healthy work-family balance.
3. **Practice Self-Care:**
   - ❖ You cannot pour from an empty cup. Taking care of your physical and mental well-being is essential for handling the stresses of both work and family life. Incorporate regular exercise, hobbies, and downtime into your routine to recharge.

The Role of Time Management

1. **Prioritize Tasks:**
    * ❖ Time management becomes crucial in balancing work and family. Start by identifying which tasks are urgent and which can be delegated or postponed. Use tools such as to-do lists or time-blocking techniques to ensure your most important tasks are completed.
2. **Be Present in the Moment:**
    * ❖ Whether you're at work or at home, focus on being fully present. When you're working, concentrate on tasks without distractions, and when you're spending time with family, give them your full attention. This focus increases productivity and allows for deeper connections with your loved ones.

Creating Meaningful Family Moments

1. **Celebrate Small Wins:**
    * ❖ Life is full of small victories, both at work and at home. Celebrate these moments, whethepr it's a promotion, a completed project, or your child's

achievements. These celebrations
strengthen bonds and bring a sense
of joy and accomplishment to family
life.

2. **Involve Your Family in Your Work
    Journey:**
    - ❖ Share aspects of your work life with
      your family. Let your children know
      what you do and how your work
      benefits the family. It helps them
      understand your responsibilities and
      appreciate the effort you put into
      your career.

Maintaining a Long-Term Perspective

Balancing work and family is not a one-time task
but an ongoing process. It requires adjustments and
flexibility as children grow and work demands
evolve. Remember, there may be periods when
work demands more attention, and times when
family takes precedence. The key is maintaining a
long-term perspective—recognizing that balance is
about giving your best to both over time, rather than
achieving perfection at any given moment.

Chapter 15: Teenage Years

"There is no such thing as a perfect parent. So just be a real one." –Sue Atkins

Navigating the teenage years requires a nuanced understanding of adolescent development. This stage of parenting brings both challenges and joys, as teenagers seek independence while still needing guidance and support. Parents must focus on fostering effective communication, helping teens navigate peer pressure, and encouraging autonomy while providing a secure foundation for their growth.

Fostering Independence from Early Childhood

Encouraging independence in children is a cornerstone of effective parenting. From an early age, parents can help their children develop autonomy, resilience, and a sense of responsibility. Laying the foundation for independence is a gradual process, and this chapter outlines how to do so from early childhood through adolescence.

Understanding Developmental Stages

Recognizing that independence evolves with each developmental stage is crucial for providing appropriate support. During early childhood, independence may mean small tasks like dressing themselves or making simple choices. In adolescence, it expands into decision-making, managing time, and preparing for adult responsibilities. This section delves into age-appropriate expectations, highlighting how parents can adjust their support to match their child's growing capabilities.

Creating a Safe Environment

A secure and supportive environment is the cornerstone of fostering independence. For young children, this means creating a space where they can safely explore and make choices within boundaries. As teens grow, providing emotional safety—where they feel free to express themselves and take calculated risks—is equally important. This section emphasizes the balance between safety and freedom as children navigate new experiences.

Encouraging Decision-Making

One of the best ways to foster independence is by empowering children to make decisions. For younger children, this could involve choosing their clothes or deciding what activity to do. As they mature, they can be included in bigger decisions, such as selecting extracurricular activities or planning their schedule. This section provides practical strategies for encouraging decision-making, which builds confidence and responsibility.

Teaching Life Skills

Life skills are essential for self-sufficiency. For young children, these skills start with basic tasks such as brushing teeth or organizing toys. As teens, life skills expand to managing money, cooking, and handling responsibilities like balancing schoolwork and social life. This chapter outlines the gradual process of teaching life skills, allowing children to grow into capable, independent individuals.

Balancing Support and Guidance

As children grow, they need both support and the opportunity to learn from their experiences. Striking a balance between guidance and giving space for trial and error is crucial. Allowing teens to take responsibility for their actions while knowing they have a safety net builds resilience. This section explores how parents can find that balance, offering support when necessary while encouraging autonomy.

Promoting Problem-Solving Skills

Critical thinking and problem-solving are key components of independence. From a young age, parents can encourage children to find solutions to their challenges, whether it's a puzzle or a social dilemma. For teens, the stakes are higher, and problem-solving may involve managing relationships, academics, or navigating peer pressure. This section provides insights on fostering resilience and adaptability, helping teens to tackle issues on their own.

Encouraging a Growth Mindset

Instilling a growth mindset in children is fundamental to their development. By praising effort and perseverance rather than just outcomes, parents can teach their children that mistakes are learning opportunities. This chapter discusses the importance of resilience and how to encourage children to embrace challenges as part of their journey toward independence.

Gradual Release of Responsibility

As children demonstrate readiness, parents can gradually release more responsibilities to them. For young children, this may involve handling small chores or managing their homework. By the teenage years, this expands into larger tasks such as managing their time, responsibilities, or even part-time jobs. This chapter outlines a step-by-step approach to gradually relinquishing control, allowing teens to handle greater responsibilities as they grow.

Cultivating Self-Esteem

A strong sense of self-esteem is critical to fostering independence. Parents play a key role in building their child's self-confidence by acknowledging their achievements and efforts. This section explores

strategies for nurturing self-esteem and providing
positive reinforcement to encourage teens to take
initiative and make independent decisions.

Modeling Independence

Children learn by observing their parents. Modeling
behaviors such as problem-solving, self-reliance,
and responsibility sets an example for teens to
follow. This chapter discusses the importance of
parents demonstrating independence and autonomy,
offering a role model for their children as they
develop similar traits.

Building Open Communication

Communication is the foundation of a supportive
relationship between parents and teens. As children
grow, maintaining open lines of communication
becomes even more important. Teens need to feel
heard, understood, and respected as they navigate
new challenges and experiences. This section
emphasizes how to foster open dialogue, allowing
teens to express themselves freely while receiving
guidance.

Acknowledging and Respecting Individuality

Each child is unique, and fostering independence
requires an understanding of their individuality.
Recognizing their strengths, interests, and personal
pace is vital for offering the right kind of support.

This chapter provides guidance on respecting a child's distinct needs and preferences, tailoring parenting approaches to their individuality.

Celebrating Milestones

As children grow, acknowledging their achievements fosters independence. Whether it's learning to ride a bike or graduating from high school, celebrating milestones reinforces their sense of accomplishment. This section explores how to meaningfully recognize and celebrate your child's journey toward independence, encouraging continued growth.

Adapting Strategies to Changing Needs

As children transition into adolescence, their needs evolve. This chapter highlights the importance of adapting parenting strategies to align with the changing dynamics of teenage development. Flexibility in parenting is key to supporting teens as they navigate new challenges, take on more responsibilities, and grow into independent young adults.

Nurturing Independence in the Long Term

Fostering independence is a long-term investment in a child's future. This concluding section provides a holistic view of the enduring impact that supportive parenting has on a child's autonomy, confidence, and ability to navigate adulthood successfully.

Parents are reminded of the lifelong value of
nurturing independence, with patience, guidance,
and love.

Chapter 16: Empty Nest Syndrome

"When your child is in the midst of a meltdown, remember that they are not giving you a hard time, they are having a hard time."

– Dr. Laura Markham

The transition to an empty nest is a significant milestone in the parenting journey. This chapter prepares parents for this inevitable shift, offering guidance on rediscovering personal interests, nurturing relationships, and embracing the next chapter of parenthood with resilience and optimism.

Understanding Empty Nest Syndrome

Empty Nest Syndrome is a psychological phenomenon that parents often experience when their children leave home, typically to pursue higher education, work, or start their own families. This stage of life can represent a significant transition for parents, marking the end of their primary role as caregivers and the beginning of a new chapter with an "empty nest."

Emotional Impact

When children move out, parents may experience a range of emotions, including sadness, loneliness, and a sense of loss. The home that was once bustling with the activities of a full household may suddenly feel quiet and empty. It's important for parents to acknowledge these feelings as a natural part of the transition. Sharing experiences with friends or other parents who are going through similar changes can help alleviate feelings of isolation.

Identity Shift

For many parents, a significant portion of their identity is tied to their role as caregivers. When children leave, parents may grapple with questions about their purpose and sense of self-worth. This period often requires a reevaluation of one's identity, and parents are encouraged to explore their personal interests and goals. Engaging in activities that bring joy and fulfillment can help reestablish a sense of identity outside of parenting.

Relationship Changes

The departure of children can also affect the dynamics between spouses or partners. Some couples may face an "empty nest crisis" as they adjust to a quieter home and changes in daily routines. It's essential for couples to communicate openly about their feelings during this transition. Couples may find it beneficial to schedule regular date nights or engage in shared activities to strengthen their relationship and navigate this new phase together.

Coping Strategies

To cope with Empty Nest Syndrome, parents can explore new hobbies, invest time in personal development, and focus on nurturing their relationships. Here are a few practical coping strategies:

- **Rediscover Hobbies**: Take up activities you've always wanted to try, whether it's painting, gardening, or learning a musical instrument.
- **Personal Development**: Enroll in classes or workshops that interest you, allowing for both personal growth and social interaction.
- **Nurture Relationships**: Spend time reconnecting with friends or family members you may have neglected while raising your children.

Maintaining open communication with children is crucial, sharing feelings and experiences during this transitional period, even if they are miles apart.

Positive Aspects

While Empty Nest Syndrome is often associated with negative emotions, it can also bring positive aspects. Parents may rediscover the freedom to pursue their interests, travel, or enjoy more quality time with their partners. This newfound freedom allows parents to embrace opportunities they may have postponed while raising their children, offering a chance for adventure and new experiences.

Parental Reflection

This stage of life provides an opportunity for parents to reflect on their parenting journey. Celebrating achievements—both theirs and their children's—can be empowering. Parents can take this time to reassess their goals for the future and consider new aspirations that excite them. Journaling about their experiences can serve as a therapeutic outlet and provide clarity on their next steps.

Staying Connected

Staying connected with adult children is crucial during this transition. Thanks to technology, regular communication through phone calls, video chats, and visits can help bridge the physical gap and strengthen emotional bonds. Parents can establish routines, such as weekly check-ins or family game nights via video calls, to maintain a sense of togetherness.

Professional Support

If the emotional impact of Empty Nest Syndrome becomes overwhelming, seeking professional support, such as counseling or therapy, can be beneficial. Talking through feelings and receiving guidance can help parents navigate this challenging period. Therapists can provide coping strategies tailored to individual needs and facilitate a healthier transition.

Embracing Change

Understanding and acknowledging the emotions associated with Empty Nest Syndrome is essential for adapting to this life transition. By embracing change, parents can discover new opportunities for personal growth and fulfillment in the later stages of their lives. This chapter emphasizes the importance of resilience and optimism, encouraging parents to view this phase as a new beginning rather than an end.

Chapter: 17 Raising Career-Ready Kids – A Decade-by-Decade Guide

"At the end of the day, the most overwhelming key to a child's success is the positive involvement of parents."   *– Jane D. Hull*

In today's rapidly changing world, preparing children for a successful career means not only equipping them with knowledge but also fostering adaptability, resilience, and self-awareness. This chapter offers a roadmap for guiding children through each decade of their early life, helping them cultivate the skills and mindset needed for lifelong success.

Ages 0-10: Foundation Building – Curiosity and Character

Goals: Develop curiosity, resilience, a love of learning, and a strong ethical foundation.

1. **Encourage Curiosity and Exploration**
   * Let children explore diverse interests through activities and play. Introduce them to new experiences and foster curiosity by answering their questions and stimulating their imagination.
   * Encourage reading, storytelling, art, and nature exploration to broaden their understanding of the world.
2. **Character and Values Formation**
   * Teach honesty, empathy, and responsibility. Reinforce these traits by modeling them in everyday situations and encouraging thoughtful actions.

❖ Allow children to experience and learn from small challenges, building resilience and the ability to handle setbacks.

3. **Learning Basic Skills**
   ❖ Introduce problem-solving and critical thinking through games, puzzles, and hands-on activities.
   ❖ Encourage teamwork and collaboration with other children to enhance social skills and foster a sense of cooperation.

Ages 10-20: Discovering Strengths and Interests

Goals: Identify strengths, build self-confidence, and encourage practical goal-setting.

1. **Encourage Self-Discovery and Personal Interests**
   ❖ Guide your child toward identifying their interests and strengths through clubs, extracurricular activities, hobbies, and volunteer work.
   ❖ Avoid pressuring them to follow only one path; instead, support exploration to help them discover their passions.
2. **Cultivate Accountability and Goal-Setting**
   ❖ Teach your child to set and achieve small goals, which builds a habit of achievement and accountability.

- ❖ Encourage them to develop routines that include study time, hobbies, and self-care to build a balanced approach to productivity.

3. **Academic and Soft Skills Development**
   - ❖ Emphasize the importance of academic skills while nurturing soft skills like communication, empathy, leadership and teamwork.
   - ❖ Encourage part-time work, internships, or volunteer experiences as they approach later teenage years to help them gain real-world insights.

4. **Mentorship and Guidance**
   - ❖ Foster relationships with mentors, whether through school, family or community, who can provide guidance and inspire future goals.
   - ❖ *Enroll them for the extra-curricular activities to Train , Coach and Mentor others in future like – Public Speaking, Memory technique , Meditation , Yoga and breathing technique, PPT presentation through various online platforms, Social Media creator (through which they can earn in future, but not just consumer to waste time on social media)*

❖ Support them in understanding
   different career options, without
   imposing limitations on their
   aspirations.

Ages 20-30: Building Career Skills and Self-Reliance

Goals: Encourage career exploration, practical experience, and decision-making skills.

1. **Guide Through Career Choices and Pathways**
   ❖ Offer support as your child selects a
      college major, trade, or other career
      path, focusing on the balance
      between passion and practicality.
   ❖ Help them understand the
      importance of adaptability in today's
      work environment by discussing
      alternative pathways, continuous
      learning, and lateral career moves.
2. **Encourage Real-World Experience**
   ❖ Encourage internships,
      apprenticeships, or entry-level jobs
      to build experience and discover
      workplace preferences.
   ❖ Support them in networking and
      forming connections that may lead to
      future job opportunities.

3. **Teach Financial Responsibility**
    - ❖ Encourage financial independence through budgeting, saving, and understanding investments to build a solid financial foundation.
    - ❖ Discuss the importance of managing debt and prioritizing long-term financial health.
4. **Cultivate Resilience and Coping Mechanisms**
    - ❖ Emphasize resilience in dealing with career uncertainties, such as job changes or market shifts.
    - ❖ Teach adaptability and a positive mindset, showing how to learn from setbacks and find growth opportunities.

Ages 30 and Beyond: Continuous Growth and Lifelong Learning

Goals: Reinforce adaptability, encourage ongoing education, and support career and personal growth.

1. **Support Lifelong Learning and Skill Development**
    - ❖ Encourage your child to pursue further education, certifications, or

skill development to remain competitive in their field.

* ❖ Discuss the importance of staying informed about industry trends and seeking opportunities for growth.

2. **Encourage Work-Life Balance and Well-Being**
   * ❖ Remind your child of the importance of balancing work with personal life and maintaining physical and mental well-being.
   * ❖ Encourage them to engage in hobbies, fitness, and social activities to create a fulfilling, balanced life.

3. **Build Emotional Intelligence and Networking Skills**
   * ❖ Reinforce the value of emotional intelligence in the workplace, helping them understand the importance of empathy, teamwork, and effective communication.
   * ❖ Encourage active networking and maintaining professional relationships to support career transitions or advancements.

4. **Foster Adaptability and Goal Adjustment**
   - ❖ *Teach them to revisit and revise career goals as needed, adapting to life changes or shifts in interests and passions generated in the previous decade.*
   - ❖ Encourage them to seek a career that aligns with their evolving values, which may involve career shifts or a new path entirely.

Every child's path to success will look different, but instilling a strong foundation in values, adaptability, and lifelong learning can empower them to pursue a fulfilling and prosperous career. By following this structured decade-by-decade guidance, parents can give their children the tools to thrive in whatever future they choose to create.

This structure gives clear, actionable steps at each life stage, helping children gradually build the skills, values, and resilience needed for a successful career. Let me know if you'd like more detail in any section!

Here are **10 essential skills to nurture in children**, aligning with each life stage in the chapter to help them thrive and succeed in their future careers:

1. Critical Thinking and Problem-Solving

- **Why it's important:** Critical thinking allows kids to approach challenges logically, assess options, and make sound decisions. Problem-solving skills foster creativity and resourcefulness in overcoming obstacles.
- **How to develop it:** Encourage curiosity and analytical thinking with puzzles, games, and open-ended questions. Teach them to break problems into manageable steps and evaluate possible solutions.

2. Emotional Intelligence (EQ)

- **Why it's important:** EQ enhances self-awareness, empathy, and interpersonal skills, all of which are crucial for effective teamwork and leadership.
- **How to develop it:** Help children recognize and manage their emotions, and model empathy by listening and responding thoughtfully. Role-playing and discussions about emotions can strengthen empathy and social awareness.

3. Adaptability and Resilience

- **Why it's important:** Being adaptable equips kids to handle change and unexpected challenges with a positive outlook, an essential trait in fast-evolving careers.
- **How to develop it:** Allow kids to experience small challenges and learn from failures. Teach them to view setbacks as opportunities for growth, and praise their efforts and persistence.

4. Communication Skills

- **Why it's important:** Clear communication skills help kids articulate their ideas, work collaboratively, and build strong relationships, all key to workplace success.
- **How to develop it:** Encourage open discussions at home, involve kids in storytelling, and help them learn effective listening skills. Activities like public speaking, debates, or group projects can also strengthen communication abilities.

5. Financial Literacy

Why it's important: Financial skills enable kids to manage their money, make informed spending choices, and understand the value of saving and investing, which supports financial independence.

Building financial literacy in children can be engaging and practical with age-appropriate activities that make managing money both fun and meaningful. Here's a breakdown of ways to develop financial literacy skills across different age groups:

Ages 5-10: Foundations of Money and Saving

1. **Introduce Allowances and Earning**
   - ❖ Give children a small weekly allowance and explain that it's their money to manage. Encourage them to "earn" additional money for small tasks (e.g., helping with household chores).
   - ❖ **Activity:** Set up a "piggy bank" or a clear jar so they can visually see their savings grow, reinforcing the value of saving over spending.
2. **Teach Basic Spending Choices**
   - ❖ Teach them to make simple spending decisions, like choosing one toy over another. Discuss needs versus wants, showing how money can be used for things we need first and then for things we want.
   - ❖ **Activity:** When shopping, involve them in budget-conscious decisions, like comparing prices on groceries or choosing between a few snack options.

3. **Set Up a Simple Budget**
    - ❖ Introduce them to a basic budgeting system. Divide their allowance into categories like saving, spending, and donating. Show them how planning for expenses helps ensure they always have enough money for important items.
    - ❖ **Activity:** Use a simple paper chart or a mobile app like PiggyBot or iAllowance to track what they spend and save each week.
4. **Savings Goals for Special Purchases**
    - ❖ Help them set a goal for a bigger item (e.g., a game or gadget) and work out how long it will take to save for it. Discuss the importance of saving gradually and avoiding impulse purchases.
    - ❖ **Activity:** Make a "Savings Goal Chart" with milestones they can color in as they get closer to their target amount, helping them visualize their progress.
5. **Introduce Charity and Giving**
    - ❖ Teach them about giving back by setting aside a portion of their allowance for donations or gifts. Discuss how they can help others and why generosity is valuable.

Activity: Let them choose a cause or charity to donate to, and explain how even a small amount can make a difference.

Ages 15-20: Advanced Budgeting and Investing Basics

6. **Create a Realistic Monthly Budget**
   - ❖ Teach them how to manage a monthly budget, especially if they're working a part-time job. Introduce tracking for income, expenses, and savings goals.
   - ❖ **Activity:** Use a budgeting app like Mint or YNAB (You Need a Budget) to help them see exactly where their money goes each month and adjust their spending habits as needed.
7. **Introduce Banking Basics**
   - ❖ Help them open a bank account and explain how checking and savings accounts work. Teach them about debit cards, ATMs, and online banking.
   - ❖ **Activity:** Take them to the bank to open a student checking account, or guide them through using a bank's mobile app to check their balance and make small deposits.

8. **Teach the Power of Compound Interest**
   - ❖ Explain the basics of interest and how it works in savings and investments. Show them how money grows over time with compound interest, emphasizing the benefits of saving early.
   - ❖ **Activity:** Use a compound interest calculator to show them potential savings growth over years. A simple example (e.g., saving $10 weekly) can help illustrate how small amounts add up significantly over time.
9. **Introduce Responsible Borrowing**
   - ❖ Explain credit basics, including how loans, interest rates, and credit scores work. Discuss borrowing only when necessary and paying back on time to avoid debt.
   - ❖ **Activity:** Create a mock scenario where they "borrow" from you and pay it back in small installments, showing how interest might make the amount increase if they don't pay on time.

Ages 20 and Beyond: Real-World Money Management

10. **Teach About Investments and Retirement Savings**

- Explain the fundamentals of stocks, bonds, and mutual funds. Introduce the concept of retirement savings accounts like a Roth IRA or a 401(k), emphasizing the long-term benefits of investing early.
- **Activity:** Help them set up a small investment account (with parental guidance if they're under 18) to learn about basic investing, or use stock simulation apps (like Investopedia's simulator) to practice investing in a risk-free environment.

6. Time Management and Organization

- **Why it's important:** Good time management helps kids prioritize tasks, meet deadlines, and avoid stress. It's crucial for maintaining productivity in both school and career.
- **How to develop it:** Teach children to set daily routines and use planners or digital tools for organizing tasks. Encourage them to break tasks into smaller steps, set deadlines, and focus on completing each step.

7. Creativity and Innovation

- **Why it's important:** Creativity drives problem-solving and allows kids to think outside the box, an increasingly valuable skill in the innovation-driven job market.

- **How to develop it:** Support activities that spark imagination, like art, music, science experiments, or creative writing. Encourage them to come up with new ideas and solutions in daily activities.

8. Collaboration and Teamwork

- **Why it's important:** Teamwork is essential in nearly every career; learning to collaborate helps kids work effectively with others, respect diverse perspectives, and contribute to shared goals.
- **How to develop it:** Engage them in group activities, sports, and projects that require cooperation. Teach them how to share responsibilities, communicate constructively, and resolve conflicts respectfully.

9. Decision-Making and Accountability

- **Why it's important:** Strong decision-making skills empower kids to make informed choices, take responsibility for their actions, and learn from their outcomes.
- **How to develop it:** Encourage kids to make age-appropriate decisions and discuss the potential outcomes of their choices. Reinforce accountability by encouraging them to take ownership of their actions.

10. Goal-Setting and Self-Motivation

- **Why it's important:** Setting goals helps kids focus on long-term objectives, while self-motivation drives them to achieve those goals, fostering a sense of purpose and discipline.
- **How to develop it:** Teach kids to set small, achievable goals and celebrate milestones. As they progress, introduce more ambitious goals and help them plan the steps required to reach them, reinforcing the rewards of self-driven accomplishments.

ABOUT THE AUTHOR

Minakshi Panda is a distinguished professional with a successful career in both banking and education, holding a master's degree in Mathematics. Her expertise spans a wide range of fields, having received advanced training from top mentors across India and internationally. Minakshi has developed a deep understanding in areas such as spirituality, parenting, leadership, motivation, personal finance, and self-development. Drawing from her extensive experiences and insights gained through numerous books, trainings, and workshops, she now seeks to share her profound knowledge with a wider audience through this book.

Driven by a passion to offer valuable, real-world insights, Minakshi's goal is to help readers benefit from the practical wisdom she has cultivated. With an ambitious yet noble mission, she aims to empower 100,000 parents to raise their children for success in today's competitive landscape, providing them with tools and perspectives shaped by her wealth of experience and dedication.

*"Man-naathah Shri Jagannathah Mat-guru-shri
jagad-guruhu. Mad-atma sarva-bhutatma tasmai
Shri Gurave Namah."*
*-My Lord Jagannath is the Lord of Universe; My
teacher is the teacher of the entire universe; and
my Self is the Self of all. My salutations at the lotus
feet of such a Guru, who has revealed such
knowledge to me.*